I love reading

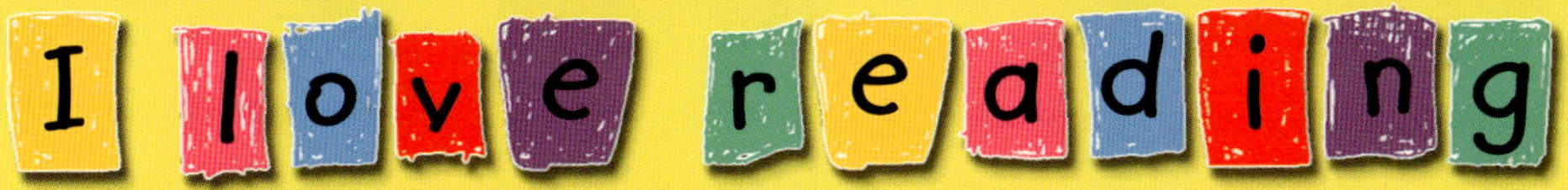

Amazing Supercars

by Frances Ridley

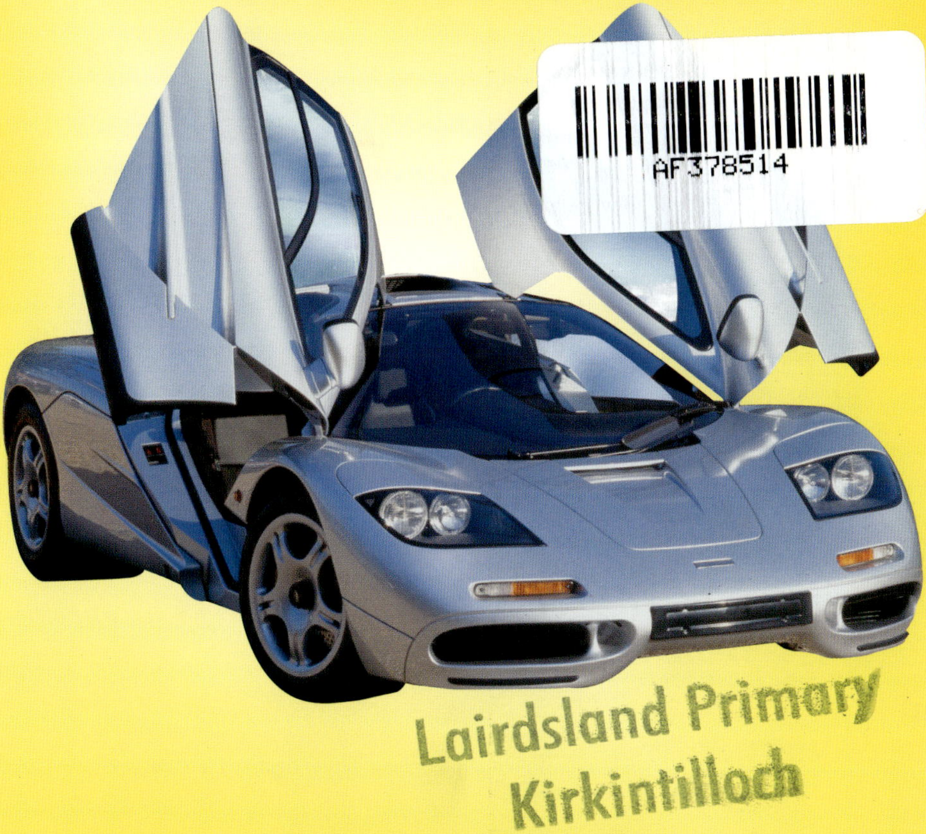

ticktock

Contents

Words in **bold** are explained in the glossary.

Copyright © ticktock Entertainment Ltd 2008
First published in Great Britain in 2008 by **ticktock Media Ltd.**,
Unit 2, Orchard Business Centre, North Farm Road,
Tunbridge Wells, Kent, TN2 3XF

We would like to thank: Penny Worms, Alix Wood and the National Literacy Trust.

ISBN 978 1 84696 773 3

Printed in China

A CIP catalogue record for this book is available from the British Library.

Picture credits: b=bottom; c=centre; t=top; r=right; l=left
All images Car Photo Library-www.carphoto.co.uk, except: Alamy: 3b, 4-5c, 5tr, 20-21c;
Auto Express: 8-9c, 9tr; www.bugatti-cars.de: 21tr

Every effort has been made to trace the copyright holders, and we apologise in advance for any unintentional omissions. We would be pleased to insert the appropriate acknowledgements in any subsequent edition of this publication.

Lamborghini Murcielago

The Murcielago's engine is behind the driver's seat. It has a top speed of 330 km/h.

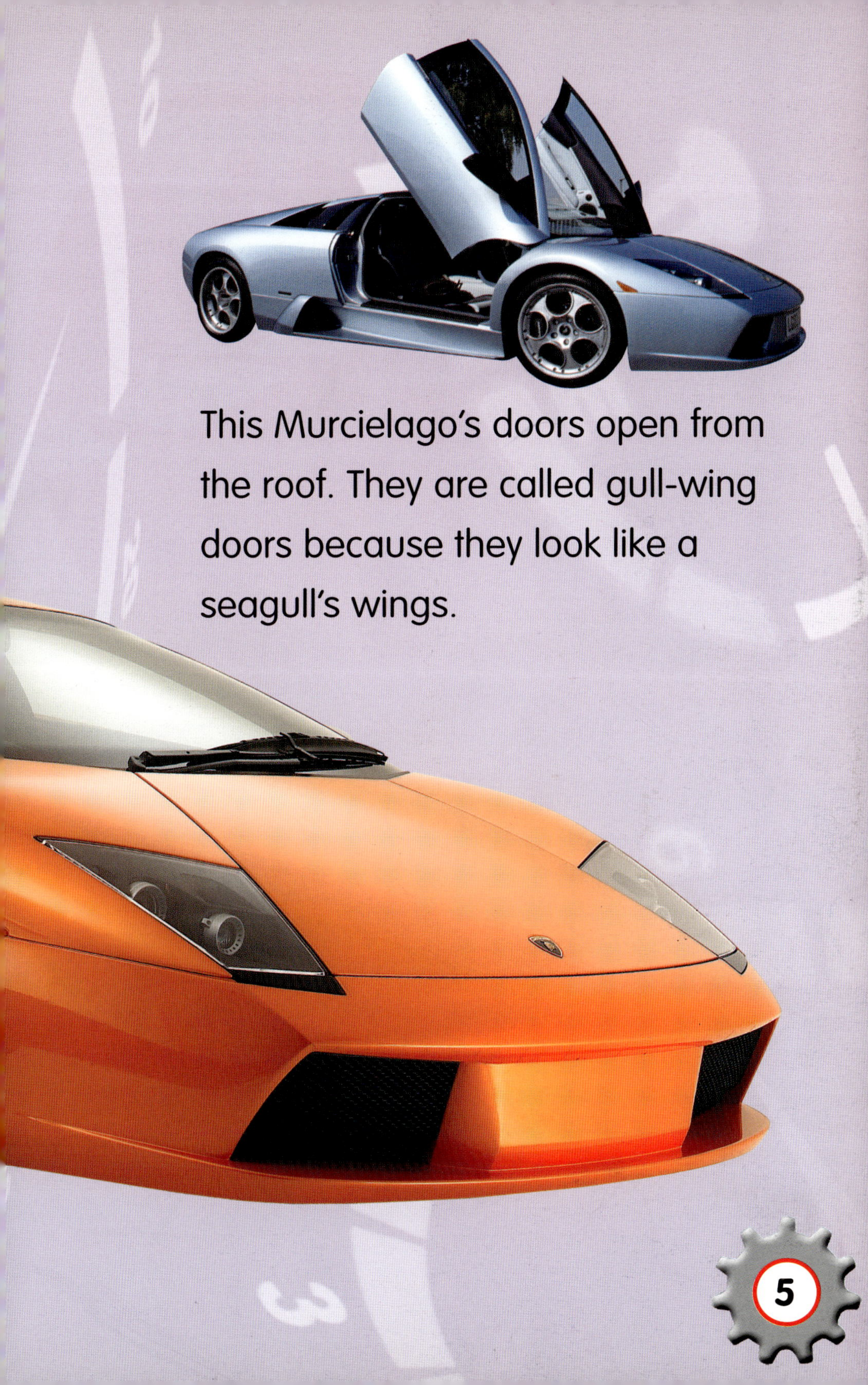

This Murcielago's doors open from the roof. They are called gull-wing doors because they look like a seagull's wings.

Bugatti EB110

The EB110 was named after Ettore Bugatti who started the Bugatti company.

6

Its body is made of **carbon fibre**. This makes it very light. Its **dashboard** is made of wood, like an old-fashioned sports car!

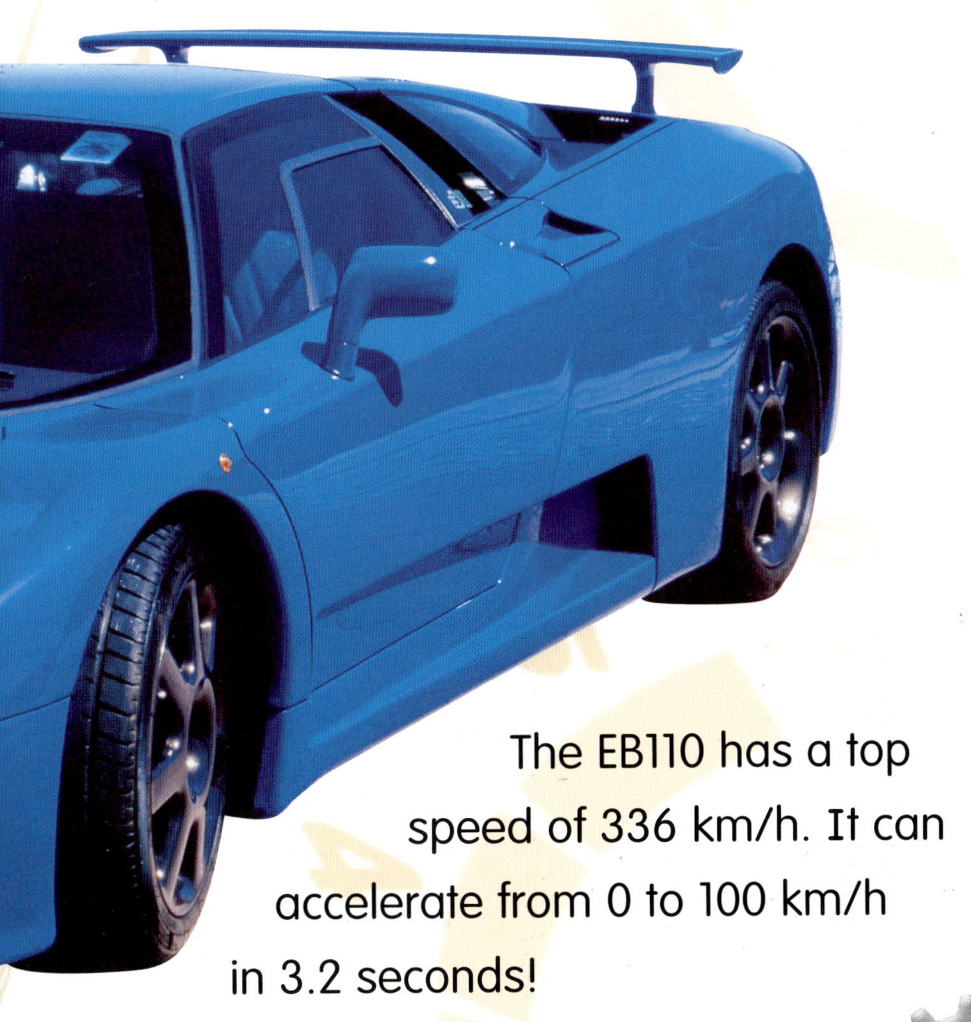

The EB110 has a top speed of 336 km/h. It can accelerate from 0 to 100 km/h in 3.2 seconds!

Noble M15

This supercar has a twin-turbo engine. It can accelerate from 0 to 97 km/h in 3.3 seconds.

8

The Noble M15
has a top
speed of
297 km/h.
It also has
satellite
navigation,
so the driver will
never get lost!

The Noble M15 was made
for everyday use. It has soft
leather seats and lots
of luggage space.

Chrysler Viper GTS

The Viper GTS replaced the Dodge Viper. The Dodge Viper only came in red or yellow. The Viper GTS comes in lots of colours, but all the cars have stripes!

The Viper GTS has an enormous V10 engine. This kind of engine was designed for trucks!

Ferrari F50

Ferrari is famous for its sports cars. By 1996, it had made sports cars for 50 years. It launched the F50 to celebrate!

The F50's engine is nearly as powerful as a **Formula One** engine. The exhausts stick out of holes in the back, just like a racing car. Its top speed is 325 km/h.

Jaguar XJ220S

The XJ220S was based on a **Le Mans** racing car. It was the fastest road car of its time. Its top speed is 349 km/h.

The XJ220S has a carbon-fibre body. This makes it very light.

It is very wide for a sports car. It has a huge wing at the back.

McLaren F1

McLaren are famous for making Formula One racing cars. They wanted to make the best supercar in the world.

The F1 was the fastest road car of its time. It is still one of the most famous. Its top speed is 386 km/h.

16

The F1 was very expensive. It cost
£634,500 and took nearly two
months to make. McLaren only
made 100 F1s.

Pagani Zonda C12 S

The Pagani Zonda was launched in 2001. Its top speed is 354 km/h. 'Zonda' is the name of a fast wind.

18

The Pagani Zonda looks like a fighter plane. It has a glass roof and an exhaust like a rocket.

It has a huge engine made by AMG. They also make racing-car engines for Mercedes-Benz.

Bugatti Veyron

The Bugatti Veyron has a top speed of 407 km/h! Only 70 have been made.

It can accelerate from 0 to 100 km/h in 2.5 seconds.

The Veyron is the most expensive **production car** in the world. Each one costs £840,000.

TVR Tuscan

The TVR Tuscan was launched in 2000. It is very light and has a huge engine. The Tuscan's top speed is 290 km/h.

You can take the Tuscan's roof off. It fits inside the large boot.

The Tuscan doesn't have door handles. You press a button under the wing mirror to get in. You twist a knob inside the car to get out!

Glossary

carbon fibre   A light material used to make cars strong.

dashboard   The panel behind the steering wheel with the speedometer.

Formula One   A famous series of motor races.

Le Mans   A famous race in France.

production car   A car designed for sale, not just for racing.

Index